THEY WALK AMO

*Unexplained tales of
ghosts and spirits from
around the Midlands*

Louise Blackburn
Charlotte Hart

Burnhart Publishing

Dedicated to Hippo-po-tamus and Richard and Andy who enjoyed the book meeting.

"All a sceptic is, is someone who hasn't had an experience yet."
JASON HAWES

CONTENTS

Little boy in the corner
TV Tricks
Hello Barbie!
You've met Mrs Kelly
Come in Sam!
What man?
Stop being lazy!

The Grey Lady of Dudley
The lady in fancy dress
The grey lady of Warley Woods
Grey Lady Hitchhiker
The Black Patch Ghostly Lady
The Grey and Lavender lady

HISTORIC HALLS - 127
Ghostly Great Barr Hall
Phantom Coach and Horses
The most haunted Hall in Brum?

HIGHWAYMEN - 138
New Hall Cavalier
Spooked on the sofa
Phantom Riders
Chester Road
Boldmere Gibbet
Time slip?

GHOSTLY ANIMALS - 145
Clever cat
The fox of Coseley Moor
Sutton Park has a Royal Visitor!
Ben the dog
Merrions Wood Cryptoid

Black Shuck on the Beacon

PREFACE

They say that most of us will experience something we can't explain at some point in our lives. For some, it'll be a one-off, random event but for many, they'll be regular occurrences.

So, we asked people living across the Midlands to share their paranormal experiences and tales of the unexplained with us. They didn't disappoint.

We have collected stories in a variety of ways and presented them here... there have been no validity checks because how you can you prove the unknown? If people tell us it's happened, that's good enough for us. It's up to you to decide how much of it you believe!

With thanks to Dean Borgazzi for the cover photo and Greg Dando for the artwork.

INTRODUCTION

A lot of people have a spooky tale to tell. This might be a personal story of something that has happened to them. It might be a story from a family member that has been passed down generations. It might also be a snippet of a story that has been talked about for many years and entered the local folklore.

For some they can be a source of comfort while some might send a spine-chilling tingle down the neck. People don't even need to believe in ghosts or spirits to have a tale to tell. There can be something entertaining in a ghost story, even if you don't think there is life after death.

This book is an eclectic collection of stories that we received anonymously through our website, emails or had told to us personally. It contains very personal stories from lost loved ones and the comfort that a visit from the other side can bring, spooky goings on in streets and hospitals. It also contains some local history and historical ghost stories that relate to sites around the Midlands.

If you have a story that you would like to share with us we would love to hear it.

You can email us on
burnhartpublishing@gmail.com

We really hope you enjoy this book and thank you for reading.

SPOOKY STREETS

The Midlands. like many areas of the United Kingdom, carries its history on its street.

Take a walk through many of our cities, towns or villages and you can easily stumble across buildings from many different periods of time.

Despite the passage of time, our streets seem to hold onto the history not just in the buildings that sit on them but somewhere within the fabric of them.

The events that impacted upon them seem to linger and punch through hundreds of years of history to frighten an innocent passerby.

THE MYSTERY MONK OF FORGE LANE

There is overwhelming speculation from many that they have 'sensed' something in Forge Lane, off the Newton Road in West Bromwich.

A young man was driving down the road late at night and had just reached a section where trees form a tunnel on either side of the road. Up ahead - he estimates about 150 yards away - he saw someone standing in the middle of the road. This is strange, as anyone who has driven down Forge Lane will know it has no pavement and is a very fast road.

The driver started to slow down feeling increasingly worried about who he was driving towards. As he gets nearer he realises that the figure is wearing a brown robe. But there is no face and there are no feet!

The writer states: "And almost as if he 'sensed' that I was coming closer, he literally drifted to the side of the road, into some nearby bushes and then just completely vanished. I barely maintained my composure enough to finish driving to the end of the road, where I managed to park up as I was so shaken."

The writer was adamant that he had seen the apparition of a monk and on carrying out some research found out that there had been a Monastery in the area which was dissolved in 1525 after a very turbulent history.

Could it be that this turbulence has led to the ghost of a monk to walk the land of Sandwell Valley? Others certainly believe this to be the case.

Lisa said she had heard about a ghostly car on Forge Lane. "My old teacher told me a car was driving towards him in the dark and as it passed him and took the bend he heard an almighty crash and smash," she described. "Thinking the car had been in an accident he quickly stopped and turned back - but there was nothing there, only blankness. No car, no crash, no headlights. Anywhere!"

Lisa C backs up the monk stories. "I've been down that road and twice, at exactly the same place, I've seen a ghost. My friend's son was with me the once and we were really shaken. The other time, I was with my grandad and a figure run out in front of us and then just disappeared. No way on earth was this a living person and there was nowhere to have come from, no paths or anything."

She says her mum has also experienced something on the road: "She saw an old man many years ago, late at night. They turned around and there was no-one to be seen, despite the fact he had been

walking in the middle of the road towards oncoming traffic."

Dandy Mandy described seeing the 'monk' on the road. She said: "I used to drive down Forge Lane regularly. One night, I was coming through about 1am and I saw him standing at the side of the road. I squinted my eyes, looked back and he had vanished. It did spook me out - I even looked behind me to see if he was sitting on my back seat."

Marie James says she had a similar experience around 2006. She explains: "Me, my daughter, her friend and her mum were driving down there late at night because the kids loved it. Anyway, just after the bend by the graveyard my daughter and her friend started screaming just as I caught a glimpse of a monk standing by the side of the road. They both said they had seen the same thing; a monk in a white robe standing with his arms folded."

Paul Swift says he saw the monk more than 30 years ago on nearby Newton Road: "Both me and the wife saw it, as plain as day, floating on the side of the road."

Natalie Stevens says her father was night fishing at the pool at Forge Lane, situated within Sandwell Valley: "Him and his mate saw a monk - he said he'd never packed his things up so quickly!" While Susan Kokomo Lamb says her brother saw a monk there, also during a night fishing trip, when he was a teenager.

Neil Greenhill said his father had also experienced the 'monk' while fishing at night. He explained: "My dad is 77 and used to fish in the pool at Forge Lane when he was a lad. He claims he saw the ghost of a monk while him and his mate were night fishing there and they both ran off without collecting up their gear beforehand.

"Sometime ago, when excavation work was being carried out around the old monastery, the body of an old monk was found who, according to local legend, was cast out of the monastery for something he'd done and couldn't be buried in the grounds.

Apparently, his body was interned at the graveyard at the old church."

After this, all the bones from the site are believed to have been re-interned in the church at the top of Newton Road.

David Halliday said there had been a lot of rumours about a monk in the 1960s. "The dare was was camp overnight in Sandwell Valley," he added.

A man who used to work for the Environment Agency, which had its depot on Forge Lane, says sightings of monks were commonplace. He writes: "Behind the depot was the River Tame and Sandwell Valley car park. I heard off a local that the apparition of a monk was seen next to the river quite often and, thinking nothing of it, I carried on with my work. A couple of months later, October or November time, we had some floods.

"Being on the flood defence side of the Environment Agency, I was on call and was checking levels at the dragons teeth in the river (concrete blocks to displace flow energy).

"I came from the depot into the car park and in the headlights, about 100 yards away, I saw someone standing on the bridge. I shouted to them 'don't jump' as I alerted my mate who was undoing the height barriers and he asked what I was talking about. There was no-one there! So I jumped in my vehicle and drove over to the river and in the driving rain I saw the figure on the path. I went to approach it and it vanished into the trees.

"I've never seen it again but have heard stories of sightings."

Georgina Jones says she saw a 'ghost monk' about three miles away from Forge Lane around 1997, on West Bromwich Expressway heading towards the motorway. "I'm not really into spirits and stuff but I know what I saw," she said.

"It was only about 3pm and I was just returning home from college. I saw a monk in a habit at the side of the road. I laughed at first but then I turned back for a second look he had vanished. I didn't know much about the monastery around there at the time so I don't think I had any reason to imagine it. Two friends in the car with me also saw him. We all laughed at the times, but thinking back it was really strange."

Katie Louise reported driving down the road and seeing what looked like a chopped-off hand in the middle of the road.

Darren Dale wrote that he had never heard of anything spooky happening on the road, until his daughter had a car accident.
He said: "It was early November 2016 and my daughter had just dropped off her boyfriend, now husband, at work. She was driving down this road towards Newton Road and on the nasty bend, just after the golf course, the car suddenly veered into a full 180 degree turn of the road and into a tree.

After smashing all the driver's side up, the car travelled and then came to a stop.
"Two lovely people behind her called us as they had managed to get the door

open on the car and get her phone. They explained what had happened and at the time we blamed it on ice or leaves, but was it? I am a believer of life after death." Darren explained his daughter had needed hospital treatment and the car was a total write-off (pictured).

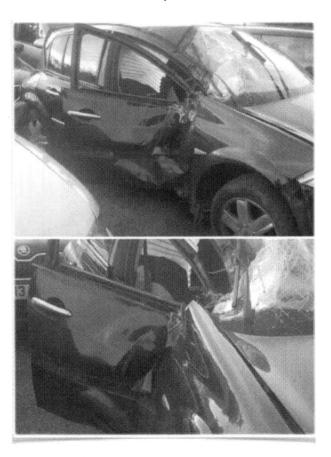

"Two days after the accident, we took her back to the scene because she had lost something out of the car, but she was adamant that she did not want to go down that lane again. Now it makes me think... was it the ice, was it the leaves or was it something else that carries on things in another life?"

Joe Davis said he almost spun out of control driving down Forge Lane at night a few years ago: "It is as if you suddenly start aqua-planing. Bear in mind that this was in the midst of summer when there had been no rain."

Barbara Humphreys wrote that Forge Lane and adjoining Camp Lane are both horrible places to drive. She said: "There have been numerous accidents down there which have been put down to speeding but I have driven on that road at night and it feels like something else has control of the car. I will no longer drive on that road if I can help it."

Parv Kaur says there have also been sightings of a 'ghostly woman' on Forge Lane. She says the vision has been blamed for a lot of accidents on the road. Jonny Bae concurred: "I've heard about card overturning after seeing a woman."

Robert Hazlehurst wrote about a spooky experience near the lake in Sandwell Valley. He said: "In January 1976, I was walking my Alsatian dog in the field next to the lake. It was bitter cold and we'd had a dusting of snow. Suddenly, I looked across too the lake and saw an old lady with a dog. She was dressed like an old hag and the dog was black.

"They just stood there looking at me but I couldn't see her face. My dog started to snarl and growl, he was shivering and his fur was standing up on his back. I put him back on his chain and looked across the lake... they were gone.

"There wasn't anywhere they could have gone to, that quickly. My dog was a large bold animal but was definitely terrified."

Samantha Hodson believes Sandwell Park Farm, which sits on the site of the old monastery in Sandwell Valley, is also haunted.
She said: "It is believed to be one of the old farmers. Every afternoon, the latch would go on the back door of the tearoom and people could hear footsteps go into the tearoom, and then into the fireplace. Many people heard it, even the non-believers!"

OLD LADY SAVED MY LIFE!

Fred from Great Barr told us that a spooky encounter had saved his life while out driving on the busy streets of Birmingham.

His tale started some what earlier than his lucky day. He explains: "I always used to see this old lady, I don't recall the first time I saw her, she was always just around. There was no rhyme or reason to when she 'appeared' but sometimes it was really frequently and sometimes I went a while without seeing her at all.

"I saw her once when I was at my nan's. I was asleep on the settee and when I came round, she was just walking round the coffee table, smiling at me. She went to sit at the armchair next to the bed and it felt like she'd pulled my hair.

"Other times I'd see and feel her sat at the bottom of my bed. I'd be playing cards with some friends at home on a Saturday night and all of a sudden she'd be sat on the bookshelf, just sat there, doing nothing. Other times I'd be eating my tea or watching TV and she'd just be there, sitting. She didn't do anything or say anything.

"I saw her for ages. She'd come, she'd go and it didn't scare me or anything. And it wasn't just in my house, she'd appear anywhere I was. "She was like a little old lady; short, petite, hair in a bun. My friends used to say that maybe it was an older relative or something, someone who had passed on, but I didn't recognise her."

But then, one night, he saw her for the very last time.

"I was driving through Birmingham, on Lichfield Road in Aston. The roads were quiet. As I approached the traffic lights at the junction, they were on green so I drove on. And as I did, I checked my rear view mirror. And there, suddenly, was the old lady. I'd never seen her in my car before. But she said 'stop'.

"It was all very quick, I hadn't expected to see her so I, without thinking, slammed my brakes on. And then, out of nowhere, at about 100mph, a car came speeding across the junction, it had jumped the red light. It would have hit me if I hadn't stopped.

"And then she was gone. That was it. I never saw her again. It's almost as if she hung around

until she was needed, then just moved on once her work was done.

"It freaks others out when I tell the story, but it happened. It was a clear as day, but as quick as a flash. Whoever she was, she saved my life.

SOMEONE IN THE ROAD

A man called Gerry was driving from Bilston to pick up his wife in West Bromwich when he experienced something peculiar in Greswold Street.

He writes: "The street lighting was not good. Given the late hour there was very little traffic and I was driving very slowly when, without warning, a woman stepped out into the road.

"I slammed on the brakes. The woman was young, gaunt and carrying a baby or young child in her arms as if they were asleep. She was wearing a light coloured coat that nearly reached the floor.

"Her face in my headlights is something that I will never forget - her expression was ghastly. I was certain I had hit her and jumped out of the car only to find she had vanished. I could smell rubber but there was no-one around, not even under the car. I got back in the car and carried on to collect my wife and drove home shaken."

MOOR LANE

Jules Sienne describes a similar story involving Moor Lane in Erdington. They wrote: "Someone thought he'd ran someone over on Moor Lane. He got out to check and there was nobody there so he drove home, albeit very shaken.

"I went to Witton Cemetery, just for a look around and I ended up standing in the part that overlooks Moor Lane, oddly enough. The air turned ice cold, as if I had walked in to a walk-in freezer and I could hear what sounded just like a hundred people whispering all at once.

"Seeing as cemeteries are a place of rest, I felt quite unnerved at how active it seemed to be. It wasn't a windy day, it was a nice bright sunny day, which is why we went. It's an eerie place to be."

A SHIMMER ON THE HEDGE

Richard, from Amington in Tamworth, told us of a very strange encounter he had in Ox Leys Road, in Wishaw, when he used to live in Sutton Coldfield.

He explains: "It was the night before the start of our holiday to Scotland and the Lakes. It was a Saturday tea time and we thought we would go and visit the grandparents down at Castle Bromwich and, from there, drive over to Shustoke to our favourite country pub 'The Griffin Inn' for a quiet drink. We thought would be a great start to our holiday.

"It was driving back through the lanes, back home to Boldmere, that we had our ghostly, or other worldly experience. We left the Griffin Pub between 8.30pm and 9pm, we had had two drinks during our visit, which was over an-hour-and-half.

"We took the usual route back home to Boldmere, a route we had travelled many times before, back through the Warwickshire countryside, through Nether Whitacre, past Aston Villa training ground at Bodymoor Heath, and then left towards the Belfry. We would pass the Belfry on the right hand side of us and then make a left towards Sutton Coldfield, along Grove Lane and across along Ox Leys Road, and finally down to the 'Anvil' pub through Sutton back to Boldmere. It's at this point that I must say that the weather was fine and clear; the light was just starting to fade as it wasn't even dusk at 9pm in August time.

"As we drove down Ox Leys Road, which is a straight hedge-lined country road, a grey shadowy figure started running down the left hand side of the verge, just a few hundred yards ahead of us. It was feature-less and seemed to shimmer as it ran about 50 yards, then shimmered across the road in front of us and carried on up the right hand side and went through the bush or between them.

"As we witnessed this apparition my wife and I wife did not utter a word for what seemed ages but was only seconds. Our brains were trying to process what we were seeing and take in… what we had just seen?

"After the stunned silence my wife asked 'did you just see that?'. I replied, 'yes, what was it?'."

Richard said, both still stunned, they continued on home, through Sutton and back to Boldmere, with the children unaware what had just happened.
He adds: "Once back at home we chatted about what we had just seen and, surprisingly, we were not frightened out of our wits. In fact, we were excited and pleased with ourselves...and sort of smug.

"We had seen something very strange and ghostly that not many people have genuinely claimed to have seen. Was it a ghost or recording of the past, or a figure that had briefly passed from its own dimension into ours. We could not explain it but it was not of this earth.

"For the very brief time my wife and I saw it our brains had trouble comprehending what we had seen. The brain is programmed to see what it sees in everyday life and when something comes along it cannot process, it seems to falter and stall.

"We were both speechless that night we saw the other worldly figure and our brains struggled to process what it had seen - it was clearly something very strange!"

A GUIDING LIGHT?

Janine, from the Black Country, says her father had told of her of a few occasions he'd encountered something 'strange'.

She wrote: "My dad (Les Willetts) used to say 'when yom jed, yom jed' but he had a few tales to tell.'

One involved a strange 'light' in the road. Janine explains: "My great grandmother Sarah Ann Cox lived with my grandparents Albert and Laura Willetts in Graingers Lane and then moved to Sutherland Road when the houses there were first built.

"Before days when children could not buy beer or cigarettes it was usually my dad or one of his siblings that my granddad used to send to the shop or the off licence to get these items.

"One night my granddad asked my dad to fetch him some cigarettes for him. Dad said he closed the back door behind him as he left for the off licence when a light shone onto the side of the house. Dad looked around to see who was shining a torch but could not see anyone.

"Dad continued to the off licence and the light followed him, dad kept looking around to see who it was but saw no one. He purchased the cigarettes and went back outside, the light shone again, followed him all the way home and when dad entered the home my grandmother Laura was crying. Dad asked why his mom was crying and my granddad said 'as soon as you closed the door your grandmother passed away'.

Janine says the family will never know if it was someone playing a trick on him or if it was her great grandmother keeping a safe eye on her grandson whilst he walked in the dark on his own.

RELATIVES

We were overwhelmed with stories about relatives visiting their loved ones after their passing. The grief of losing a loved one is a difficult and arduous process and ultimately accepting the fact you will never seem them again takes time and strength.

Studies have shown that up to six in ten bereaved people feel that there is something more after the loss of a loved one and the legacy they leave is not just memories and photos but they still feel their presence, they may hear them call out or say a phrase often uttered when they were alive, they may smell a familiar cigarette smell or much loved perfume associated with the person who has passed or even see them!

Scientists call this 'post-bereavement hallucinatory experiences' - and believe they can happen to anyone, including sceptics. These experiences are often of comfort and the next few stories may make you wonder whether it is just a mechanism of human grief or whether there is something more.

WAS BRIAN 'WATCHING' OVER ME?

Almost 50 years ago, Pauline and her first husband were living on the 12th floor of a block of flats in Smethwick with their two-year-old daughter. Next door lived a couple with a three-year-old son and a newborn baby. One day, tragedy hit which led to an experience Pauline can't quite explain.

She says: "My little girl used to play with the little boy next door. His favourite toy was his

The block of flats where Pauline lived in Smethwick shortly after it was built in 1968. She lived there from 1970 until the summer of 1972. The entire block was demolished some years later.

metal rocking horse. He used to rock it so vigorously that it would travel across the floor.

"One Sunday morning he tragically died after falling through the window. His mum asked me if I'd like the rocking horse for my daughter as she couldn't bear to keep it.

"Sitting in the kitchen having lunch one day, I heard a noise in the lounge. Peeping round the door, I noticed the rocking horse vigorously rocking across the floor. But no-one was in the room at the time and so there was no explanation for the rocking horse moving. Then, just as suddenly, it stopped dead. We couldn't believe our eyes. Needless to say, the rocking horse was thrown down the rubbish chute."

Then, she says, another experience took her by surprise: "Many years later I had been divorced and remarried. My husband collected watches and clocks, and much to my annoyance we had several clocks in every room (some of Brian's collection are pictured).

"After a long illness, Brian passed away, seven years ago. I spent his last five days and nights at his side. For this reason I decided I didn't want to see him in his coffin before the funeral.

"However, a few days before the funeral, all the clocks in the house went haywire, either 10 minutes slow or 10 minutes fast. No matter how many times I put them right, they would change again.

"My gold watch that Brian had had specially made for me also behaved in the same way. I took it to have a new battery fitted, but by the time I got home again it was 10 minutes fast. I talked about it to my youngest daughter and she said 'Mum, I think Brian wants you to go to see him'…

"So I made an appointment for a 'viewing' and I spent some time with Brian. I ended by telling him to stop messing with the clocks and my watch because it was annoying. When I got home all the clocks and my watch were correct.
"As a footnote to this. One of the clocks is a very old pendulum clock, which always chimed at four minutes to the hour, much to everyone's amusement.

"I stopped winding the chime after Brian's death, but on New Year's Eve following his funeral in November, the clock chimed six times at midday.

"I really can't explain them any more than I can explain why a robin comes to my window every Christmas morning, on my birthday and our anniversary."

WAS MY AUNTIE WORRIED ABOUT ME?

A similar tale was told by a Tamworth woman who said she felt her auntie had come to make one last check on her before she died.

The woman, who is in her 40s, explained: "I was in my mid-20s so early in the 2000s, and I was in a bad place emotionally. I had been made redundant and was going through a real bad patch.

"My auntie had cancer and my mum had been diagnosed with cancer before that so they had it at the same time.

"One day, my mum and dad went to visit my auntie to see how she was doing and when they got back, they said my auntie had asked after me a lot and had been really concerned about how I was doing. It was like I was on her mind, they said.

"That night, I was woken by someone on the bed. It was about 1am and I felt someone sit on the bottom of the bed. I looked up and saw my auntie. I jumped up and blinked and then she was gone. It really freaked me out.

"Anyway, the next morning, we were going away on holiday. My sister was driving and as we went along I found myself saying to her that I think our auntie had passed away in the night. It had been playing on my mind.

"I hadn't said anything to mum and dad at the time as they were also coming on the holiday. I didn't want my dad distracted while he was driving to meet us.

"When we all arrived at our holiday destination, I mentioned it to them... I said I thought something had happened to auntie. So my dad rang my uncle and he confirmed it, that she had died about 1am that morning.
"I think she must have been worried about me because she had been talking about me in the day. I was obviously on her mind and I think she came to see me before she passed away. I told my mum and dad about seeing her in the night and they believed me.

"I haven't really told anyone else because it really freaked me out and I worry people will I'm mad, but I know what I saw and felt. It freaked me out at the time."

TIPTOE THROUGH THE TULIPS

Tammy says a helping hand when she was having a panic attack on a bus gives her reassurance of her grandad's love.

She explains: "I lost my grandad as a toddler and I don't remember much about him apart from the fact that I was scared of him because he had Parkinson's Disease which caused him to shake a lot.

"When I was aged around 19 or 20, I was on a very packed bus and was in the middle of a panic attack because I get very claustrophobic.

"There was a man dressed very old-fashioned sitting opposite me, looking directly at me. I remember thinking he looked very much like my grandad from the photos I have seen of him.

"Anyway, he started whistling 'Tiptoe Through the Tulips' and I instantly became calm and stopped panicking. I then got off bus and looked to find where this man was sitting, but there was no-one there.

"I got home and told my mum about it, and she asked if the song had been 'Tiptoe Through The Tulips'. I was shocked and told it was. She told me that when I was a tiny baby, my grandad used to whistle that song to me to stop me from crying.

"I think of that day a lot; it was a very weird situation but it does make me happy when I think about that day. He was an amazing man from what I've heard."

TREMBLING UNDER THE COVERS

Alan, from Oldbury, said he had an encounter which he thinks may have been his parents trying to say one last goodbye.

He explains: "I had been looking after my elderly parents for a number of years until I lost my father and two years later, my mother sadly passed away. The property that we all lived at was left to me in their will and I lived there alone until I bought a flat, moved into it and sold the house very quickly.

"A month or so before I moved in to the flat, I woke up one night around 3am and lay under the blankets trying to get back to sleep, when I felt something or someone sit down on the bottom left side of my bed. I trembled under the blankets, too scared to see who or what was there until I finally dropped off to sleep again.

"A week or so later, the same thing occurred once again with me waking up during the night and feeling the bed go down at the bottom left side.
"Again, I was frightened and too scared to peer over the blankets, once again drifting back to sleep until dawns light entered the bedroom and whatever it was had disappeared.
"Was it my late parents trying to say their last goodbyes to me? That, I will never know...."

I RECOG- NISED THE LADY IN THE PHOTO

Another lady described seeing a relative sitting on her bed.

She explained: "When I was young, my sister had whooping cough and she was seriously ill. One night I woke up to see my mum sitting on the edge of her bed. The next morning, I asked my mum why she was sitting on the end of the bed. She denied she had been and said I must have been dreaming.

"Later on, however, I was looking through pictures and I saw the woman who was so like my mum. She said it was a photo of her sister who had died at an early age.

"This was the woman who had been sitting on my sister's bed while she was ill!"

YOUR PRO-GRAMME IS ON ARTHUR!

A grand-daughter wrote into tell us about Sarah Jane, her straight-talking maternal grandmother who 'didn't suffer fools'"Everything that came out of her mouth was the truth.

She adds: "On a visit to my grandmother's home not long after her son-in-law and my uncle Arthur Cartwright, who lived with her and my Aunt Ada, passed away. Aunt Ada had gone out for the night with my mom so I visited with my Aunt Daisy and started to talk about Uncle Arthur. Aunt Daisy said she bet my grandmother missed him. Gran said when something came on the TV that Uncle Arthur liked, Gran would turn and say to him 'your programme is on Arthur', then remember he was no longer there.

"Gran said she had the feeling that Uncle Arthur was still around until one night, she'd felt his presence. Gran said she turned to look at his chair and in the doorway stood Uncle Arthur. He smiled and left. Gran said she never felt his presence again after that night."

Janine says this was not the first incident that had happened to her grandmother: "Gran went on to say that when she was 12 years old and her one sister - my great aunt Emmie (Crewe) - was two years old, their mother died.

"Gran said that the doctor came down the steep steps in the house and told her that her mother had passed away. She said that she had her sleeves rolled up (as she always did), put her head in her arms that was leaning on a scrub top table and sobbed.

"Gran said at that point she heard a female's voice that she knew. The sharp tone of her voice as she called out my Gran's name: 'Sarah,

stop your crying, I'm alright where I am and you have to look after that baby upstairs'.

"Gran said she stopped crying and never cried again over her mother."

GRANDAD'S LAST FAREWELL

Phillip is still mystified by his experience as a 12 year old and still finds it strange to remember. His grandad was a lovely man and Phillip spent a great deal of time with him as a child. "He was a lovely grandad and he taught me how to fish and was a kind and loving man.

"Sadly he was diagnosed with cancer and given a very short amount of time to live."

Phillip remembers visiting him at the hospital and his family being gathered around him as he slipped into unconsciousness.

Phillip said "I whispered my final farewells and then I went home with my mom. I went to bed when we got in and finally fell asleep but at 2am woke suddenly. I don't know what woke me but I was shocked to see my grandad standing over me though!

"My grandad looked at me, smiled kindly and turned around and walked out of the bedroom door. I was stunned and then the phone rang

and broke the silence. The phone call was my dad telling my mum that grandad had passed away.

"My mom came into my room to tell me the news and I muttered that he had just seen him in the room but my mum insisted it was a dream."

Phillip says "I am still not sure I believe in the paranormal but it was either a co-incidental dream or my grandad did come to visit me one last time."

HAUNTED HOUSES

It is estimated that we spend 45% of our time at home. It is the place that we should feel safest and the only people within the walls should be those we invite in or live there. This might not always be the case for every house though.

Haunted houses form part of the folklore of ghosts. The haunted old mansion on top of the dark hill with a lightning flash for effect. The creaky old wooden stairs or an old damp cottage.

It is true to say though that even the newest of houses can have spooky goings on and this collection of stories involves your usual suburban houses from across the local area.

SPOOKY STAIRS

Rebecca, from Perry Barr in Birmingham, recalls how an unusual knock at the door made her want to hide in her bedroom.

Her first floor flat, where she lived with her partner, was only accessible via a flight of metal stairs behind a metal gate that was in the landlord's backyard.
She explains more: "It was impossible to open the gate and climb the stairs without making a noise and we always heard each other approaching as we came home or friends and family visited."

One night, Rebecca was home alone, watching TV when there was an unexpected knock at the door.

"I was watching TV quite happily and not expecting visitors at all," she said.
"Suddenly I heard someone coming up the stairs quite loudly. The footsteps stopped at the top, there was a pause and then a knock on the door! I was puzzled as I wasn't expecting visit-

ors and I hadn't heard the metal gate so I thought it might be the landlord.

"I opened the door and there was absolutely no-one there, just an empty space at the top of the stairs! I was so scared, I slammed the door, locked it and ran to my bedroom and hid there until my partner came home!

"I still really cannot understand what walked up the stairs that night and there is absolutely no way they could have run down them silently in the time it took me to answer the door."

WHAT WAS THAT WHISTLING?

A businessman from Sutton Coldfield told us about an experience his parents had as newly-weds.

The couple had just moved into an old council house they were renting in Hockley; they didn't have much money so it was all they had been able to afford. They knew that an old man had been the last person to live in there and that he had died in the back bedroom.

The couple's son explains more: "When they moved in, the bed that he had died in and all the furniture was still in the room so they chose to leave it as it was shut the door and never go in there. They decided that they would use the front bedroom which was, on the other side of the wall."

He said that his parents told him that they often got a creepy feeling while they were living there but, one particular night, it all came to a head.

"My dad was starting to build his business and was getting in late for work every night," he added.

"That night, he got in and my mom met him at the door. He immediately sensed something was different. There was a weird, vague whistling noise and my mom said the dog had been acting weird all day.

"Anyway, they went to bed and turned off the light. In the dark, the whistling got louder and louder and the bed actually started to shake. Then they looked at the wall that was adjoined to the other bedroom and they couldn't believe their eyes.

"A weird, bright shape was floating in the wall. My dad described it as 'like a square, like a child had drawn it'. It slowly floated away from the wall and stopped at the end of their bed.

"They both lay there, frightened, wondering what to do. In the end my dad suggested they try praying - so they said the Lord's Prayer. It

vanished. The bed stopped shaking and the noise stopped."
The couple moved out not long after!

THREE OR FOUR?

Kathryn, who lived in Kingstanding in the mid-2000s, said her toddler regularly used to talk to someone at the bottom of the bed during the night.

She explained: "I always felt like there was someone or something else living in the house with us. Sometimes, when my husband used to go out to work early, leaving the rest of us in bed, I used the hear footsteps walk down the hall.

"I used to shout out to my husband, asking what he'd forgotten and assuming he'd popped back for something, but there was never any reply. And if I got up to investigate, there was never anyone there.

"As my daughter reached about two-and-a-half years old, we would regularly be woken by her talking in the middle of the night. We used to get up to make sure she wasn't having a bad dream, but she used to just be sitting at the end of the bed, happily chatting away to someone.

She always seemed to be having a conversation with someone, it wasn't random words. There were pauses in her talking, like she was listening to someone's reply.

"She used to sit at the same place whenever we got up to check on her, at the foot of the bed, nearest the window.

"She never seemed to understand why we fussed about it because it was completely normal to her... we were more freaked out by it than she was. This went on for a couple of years, every now and again.

"One day, when she was aged about four or five, we told her we were going out for something to eat and she asked if we were all going. 'Yes, all three of us', I confirmed. She just looked at me confused.... asked if I meant all four of us. I explained only three of us lived there and that the three of us were going out. But she told me, confidently, that actually there were four of us living in the house and so all four of us should go out.

"We moved house not long after that and she never once woke again to talk to someone at the end of the bed in the middle of the night, thank goodness!"

LITTLE BOY IN THE CORNER

Nadine Holt, from Tamworth, says she always felt unsure about a house she lived in Polesworth, during the 1970s.

She said: "In 1970, my then husband and I moved into an old early 1900s semi. It was cheap and needed some TLC, but I felt a bit 'funny' about it. My husband asked the neighbours not to tell me if anyone had died in there as I was a bit spooked.

"One day I was in the kitchen doing the washing. I moved the old washer from the corner and connected up the hoses to the taps, washed the nappies and prepared to put them through the wringer on top.

I looked up from my wringing, momentarily, towards the corner and I saw a little boy of about eight years old. He was dressed in grey school shorts, with a school cap on his head. It was a fleeting glimpse and I pushed it away as being in my imagination.

"However, a couple of weeks later the same thing happened. Then a few more times. It was not scary, just a little boy. I asked the neighbours about it and they knew nothing.

The house in Polesworth

"When we left to move to a newer house, the neighbour told me that a little boy who had lived there died at an early age after they moved to another house!

"My elder daughter was born there and she was a baby who cried all night, every night. I often wonder if the atmosphere was something to do with it."

Nadine says the little boy wasn't the only 'visitor' to the house. She explains: "In the same house, we refurbished our front room, which turned out very well. But I was never comfortable sitting in there on my own.

"If my husband was out in the evening, I would sit in the dining room, reading, but with a dining chair under the door handle. If I had to go in there it was as if somebody was taking a deep breath and then holding it until I had gone.

"Again, upon leaving the house, my neighbour told me that the old man who had lived there had died in the sitting room. Apparently he was not a pleasant man."

But it wasn't just the house on Polesworth that Nadine says she felt 'something'. There was a hotel too…

"I booked to stay for two nights at an old coaching hotel in order to have a couple of days walking in a rural area. I went to bed the first night and as I was lying there, planning my next day's walk, someone was in the bed behind me, squeezing the breath out of me.

"I screamed and jumped out of bed, sensing a presence in the room. I phoned reception and told them I wanted to check out as there was 'something' in the room.

"They offered an alternative, thinking I meant a mouse or something. I explained and the receptionist offered to come up and escort me away and down the stairs.

"That made me think it had happened before. He begged me not to check out to travel home in the early hours, but I could not stay. I asked reception not to book any lone lady guests into that room."

TV TRICKS

Kitty told us she was convinced there was something in her house, in Perry Barr, Birmingham, after a TV flew across her daughter's bedroom.

She said: "When the children were teenagers, they both had a TV/video in their bedrooms. One Sunday morning, we were all downstairs and there a massive crash and bang in my daughter Louise's bedroom.

"We all ran upstairs into her bedroom and the TV was on the floor, on its side. It had come off the chest of drawers; it had fell and twisted in the air to land on its side. The strangest thing was that our cat was asleep on the bed and she hadn't stirred at all. When my husband picked the TV up, he saw that it had fallen with such force that it had broken the floorboards. And surprisingly, the TV still worked.

"There was no way that the TV could have come off the chest of drawer, twisted in the air and landed on its side, on its own. And to this day, we cannot explain what happened."

HELLO BAR-BIE!

Lynne also says she has a 'house that does strange things' in Tamworth. She explained: "One such time was when I thought my daughter had got out of bed in the night and was standing by my bed, as she sometimes did when she was little. I threw the quilt open and said 'come on then', indicating for her to get into my bed, but then she was gone. I went into her room to check she was okay and she was fast asleep.

"Also, my daughter had a toy Barbie table which had a working lamp and telephone which beeped to sound like a number was being dialled and a voice which said 'Hello Barbie'. This would come on at random times during the night, usually between 3-3.30am.

"Another time, I was listening to a CD and the volume went up so I turned it down. This happened twice more and the last time I said, 'pack it in', and it didn't happen again.

"Other things happened, like a mobile phone top-up card flying off a shelf when there couldn't have been a draught as there was paper on the same shelf. Also, hearing a little girl's voice shouting 'mum'.

"A man who worked at the same place as me said his mum had lived in my house as a little girl with her parents, so I asked him to ask her if a little girl had died here. She told him a little girl called Susan Shaw used to come to stay with them.

"On one visit she fell ill and was calling for her mum. It turned out she'd contracted meningitis at nine years old and later died. My own daughter got meningitis aged nine, and lived."

Lynne said her partner had also experienced 'something'.

She added: "One evening, when my partner had been upstairs, I asked him who he had been talking to. He said he'd said hello to my daughter standing in her bedroom doorway. She wasn't home but he was sure he'd seen her.

"And our dog (pictured) sometimes follows something along a wall in our living room, but nothing is there."

In addition, Lynne says that a recent experience had reminded her of something else that had happened in her house.

"I got up to go to work at 5am for my early shift, so it was dark. I saw something small and very bright fly into my bedroom close to the floor, but when I went to see what it was there was nothing there.

"It reminded me of the time when I was at home alone. We hadn't got the dog at the time, and I'd just changed my bed. When I went back into my bedroom there was an imprint on the bed and pillow as if someone had been lying on it. Strange because, as I said, I was in the house on my own."

YOU'VE MET MRS KELLY

This spooky story comes from Northfield from a former police officer called Roy.

He says: "One time, at about 3am, I was on night duty pedal cycle patrol. It was a moonless night, as I remember, and I had passed down that road on many previous occasions. My mind was in neutral reaching the end of a long night with not a lot happening.

"As I passed the row of cottages on Church Lane (sadly no longer there) on the right hand

8. NAILERS' COTTAGES, CHURCH ROAD, NORTHFIELD. c. 1936   BIRMINGHAM PUBLIC LIBRARIES

side I was aware of a light in one of the windows – not an electric light but a sort of flickering. I thought at first that it was a reflection from nearby streetlights but there were none in the immediate vicinity, so I decided to investigate.

"As I approached the cottage concerned I was aware that the light was caused by a candle flickering in the dark of the interior.

"I looked closer and saw an old woman, her hair tied up in a bun, rocking to and fro in a rocking chair. It was this rocking which was causing the flickering, as the woman kept passing in front of the candle. As I peered through the window her head turned and she looked straight at me. I waved, received no acknowledgement, remounted my bike and rode on.

"Towards the end of my tour of duty I met my friend and asked about the old lady in the rocking chair in the cottage. 'Oh', he replied, almost casually, 'you've met Mrs Kelly'."

Roy said he remarked that three in the morning was a rather late hour to be up and about – or early, depending on your viewpoint. He added: "My friend smiled and said, 'She's often around

at that time. She died about ten years ago, you
know'."

COME IN SAM!

Janine from the Black Country says her parents told her of a house they used to live in when they were first married.

"Mom and dad married in February 1951 and their first home together was a room above a shop in Surfit Hill, Cradley Heath, run by Maggie Lowe.

"My parents would often see a table setting for two, or when Maggie made a pot of tea she would lay two cups out. On seeing this, one day my mom asked Maggie if she was expecting a friend for tea. Maggie said no it was for

Sam her husband. Sam had passed away a few years earlier."

Janine says strange things would happen in their little room. She explained: "Mom said she would hear the door latch open when the door was locked, a light would flicker for no reason and items would be moved when she returned home from work. They would hear Maggie holding a one-sided conversation with her husband Sam.

"On one occasion, my mom had gone away for the weekend to earn extra money hop picking. Dad was on his own so decided to go to my grandad's who lived up nearby in Codsall Road.
"Dad was pressing his trousers when he heard the door latch open, thinking mom had come home early he turned to the door, it opened slowly, dad stood there watching as the door closed again. There was no wind around to assist the door. The latch went across and bolted the door.

"Dad said that he grabbed his trousers and shoes, ran out of the room and ran to my granddad's still putting his trousers on. He arrived at grandad's still putting his shoes on. My granddad looked at my dad and said 'you look like you have seen a ghost'. Dad turned to grandad and said 'I haven't seen one, but one just open and closed my door'."

Janine says her dad told this story to everyone and growing up, if the door blew open, dad would say 'come in Sam'.

WHAT MAN?

Janine also had a story about family friend, Derek Dunn.

She wrote: "We had family friends Derek and Ron Dunn, brothers, who grew up and lived all their lives in Quarry bank. The brothers never married or had children of their own. They loved to visit friends and family especially if they had children.

"Derek was a tease, he used to play with the children's toys and say he was not going to give them back. Derek was also a gadget man, anything new that was advertised on TV or in magazines he had to have.

"When Derek passed away his brother Ron said he could not live in the house alone so moved in with me. The last house the brothers lived in

together was bought by my niece Ruth and her family.

"Oliver was two years old and knew Ron. On every visit to me Ron would have sweets for him. But Oliver never meet Derek.
"Derek and Ron were always cold and had the heating high even in a heatwave.

"Ruth complained to her fiancé that the heating was turned up high all the time in the house and for him to stop turning it up so high. Craig said that he had not touched the heating. This happens still.

"One night, the family were all asleep upstairs when Ruth and Craig were woken up by the sound of the TV. Craig, before going to bed, always switches the TV and other appliances off at the socket, so how was it that the TV was on? When downstairs, Craig found that not only was the TV on but the Wii games were too. This has happened a few times."

Janine says that one day, Oliver was playing in his bedroom and Ruth could hear him talking to someone. She added: "Ruth put it down to an imaginary friend. Toys were out all over the room and Ruth asked Oliver to tidy up after himself. But Oliver replied 'it's not me, it's the man'. Again this was an ongoing thing. Ruth said that Oliver needed to tidy up and Oliver said, again, that it was the man who had all the toys out. Ruth asked sharply, 'what man?'. Oliver replied 'Derek'.

"Another time, when Oliver was three, Ruth's mum visited her and Oliver told his nanny that he was playing upstairs with the man and his toys. Pauline asked Oliver 'what man?'. Again, Oliver replied 'Derek'.

"So Pauline showed a photograph of both Ron and Derek and asked Oliver who the men in the picture were. Oliver looked at the photo and laughed, pointed to the picture and said that it was Ron and Derek. We were still wondering how he knew as Oliver had never met Derek, and we had not spoken about Derek in a long time.

"Then the day came when we all went to Powke Lane Cemetery to have Ron and Derek's ashes scattered. Oliver was playing around the tree and laughing and talking to someone. When we asked Oliver who he was talking to, Oliver pointed towards the tree and said in a puzzled voice, almost like why are you asking me, 'can't you see? It's Derek'.

STOP BEING LAZY!

Chris had a strange tale to tell about her house of the Pheasey Estate in Great Barr. One day, when her children were little she was lying on the bed upstairs.

Chris said "The children were playing nicely downstairs and I was having a quiet five minutes lying on the bed, I had my eyes closed but I wasn't asleep when suddenly a man shouted 'Get up now, get out of bed, DON'T BE LAZY!' It was like there was a man was shouting in my face! It really scared me and I sat straight up in bed but there was nothing there."

Chris was convinced that it was a figment of her imagination so carried on with her day and didn't tell anyone.

"A few months later I was at a gathering with neighbours. Conversation turned to the local area and a couple who lived a few doors away started discussing how they had considered moving out recently. My neighbour looked a bit embarrassed to discuss it but encouraged by her husband she told the following tale. She had recently been working nights and one day came home after a particularly busy shift. She got into bed and was just dropping off when she all of a sudden heard a man shouting at her! He was telling her to not be lazy and to get out of bed! I was so shocked to hear an almost identical experience!

"The neighbour was terrified and struggled to sleep. A couple of days later, once again after a night shift, she lay down in bed only to feel someone get into bed next to her and make a suggestive comment. The neighbour shot out of bed and absolutely terrified at this awful presence she declared that she wanted to move!"

The neighbour told Chris that they decided firstly to get the house blessed by the local vicar and this bought the visitations to a stop.

Chris added "The vicar told the family that she had been called out to a number of houses on the Pheasey Estate. The vicar felt the reason was that part of the Pheasey estate was requisitioned by British Forces in 1942 and that American soldiers were placed in the houses on the estate. She felt that as these American GIs were reaching the end of their lives and passing away that they were visiting some of their old haunts from when they were vibrant young soldiers!"

MP on duty at Entrance to Pheasey on Romney Way (10th Replacement Depot Archives)

HOSPITALS

Whole books are written on the supernatural experiences that occur with the walls of hospitals.

It is no surprise really; they see life and death in all its stages, pregnancy to birth, to illness, to the end of life. They see love, hope, grief and loss.

A number of local Midlands hospitals have stood for more 100 years watching the progress of society and it seems they have also been collecting their own collection of spirits and ghosts.

HIDE-AND-SEEK

Jules had just had a second child by C-Section at Good Hope Hospital when she encountered something she couldn't quite explain.

She had been bed-bound for a couple of days and had just started to get up and walk about a bit.

"I hobbled out of the bed and made it to the door," she explained. "I carried on going all the way down to the lifts and back again. On the way back to my room, I noticed a half moon shaped table/counter, which I never really noticed when I came out of my room.

"Just before I got to it, I saw a little girl crouching down behind it looking at me and laughing.

"I remember thinking, 'aww, she's just become a big sister and is here to see her new baby brother or sister. As I got closer to this table, she went around the back of it, like she wanted to play hide and seek so, even with all my pain, I decided to humour her. I thought she was probably bored."

Jules says that as she went round to the other side of the table to make the little girl jump, the little girl must have crawled round to the front of the table as she could no longer see her.

"I couldn't see her", she said. "I mustered up the energy to go around the whole table, three times, but she wasn't there.

"I can even remember what she was wearing - a white dress with what looked like tiny blue flowers on; white ankle socks and buckled shoes; a white, what looked hand-knitted cardigan, and her hair was blonde, long and in a curly/ringlet kind of style with a blue head-band."

The little girl had just disappeared – but was she ever really there in the first place?

THEY LOOKED MORE LIKE NUNS

Hazel also had an unexplained experience while recovering from a C-Section at Good Hope Hospital.

She said: "I was in a side ward when two nurses wearing strange hats - more like what nuns would have worn years ago - started chatting to me. They were telling me what I should do with baby, how lovely he was and how he would have a wonderful life. They said goodbye and went.

"When the usual nurse came into me she told me to do something opposite to what I'd been told, and when I questioned it, she asked 'what nurses?'

I described them to her and she thought they were some sort of religious visitors, I guessed she didn't believe me or thought I was a bit peculiar, it was very real to me and I have often wondered who they were, even after 40-odd years."

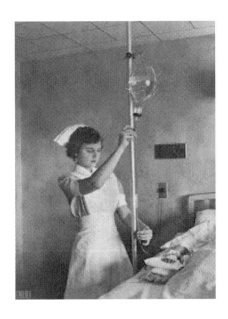

A FAMILIAR FACE ON THE HOSPITAL WARD

A niece shared a story about the experience of her Auntie Daisy in a hospital in the Black Country. She explains: "When my mom's sister Daisy became pregnant with her eldest child Stephen, she and her husband Cyril lived with his parents in Meredith Street in Cradley Heath and her father-in-law had been over the moon that Daisy was expecting a baby.

"Unfortunately, before Daisy gave birth her father-in-law passed away. Auntie Daisy said that she was in hospital after giving birth to Stephen and he was in the crib at the bottom of the hospital bed.

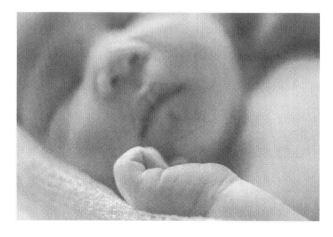

"Auntie said she was half asleep when she looked up the ward and saw a familiar figure walking towards her. She realised that the familiar figure was her father-in-law. He came close to the bed and sat on the end... Auntie Daisy said she felt the bed go down. Her father-in-law looked into the crib at the baby, then turned and smiled at her. He then got up from the bed and walked away.

"Auntie Daisy called the nurse and told her the story of what she had just experienced. The nurse replied 'you are not the first mother to experience a passed loved one come visit them when they have a baby'."

MAYBE IT WASN'T HER TIME

A business owner from Tamworth says her mum was convinced she had been visited by her nan, who had died some years earlier, when she had been ill in Good Hope Hospital.

"My mum was pregnant with me and was very poorly in hospital as she had been diagnosed with cervical cancer. She was so very very ill. I think it had been touch and go.

"She had been asleep and when she opened her eyes, her nan was sat there with her arms wide open, like she was calling her to come closer. As my mum started to move, her nan folded her arms closed across her chest, almost as if to say no, don't come close after all.

"They had been very close when her nan was alive, she had lived with her as a child."

"When my mum closed her eyes again, she was gone. My mum always says it was like her nan had to come take care of her again but had decided that it wasn't her time after all so pushed her away at the last minute."

*Good Hope was built for the Reverend Riland Bedford in 1882. Originally known as x Close, it became known as Good Hope House after a change of ownership in 1912. It was converted into an auxiliary hospital in 1943, taking in medical and post-operative cases, mostly soldiers who were moved there to convalesce. Two single-storey wards were added in the 1950s and its thought that many people have walked through those corridors - maybe not all of the earthly kind.

THEATRE
TALES

There are some wonderful theatres across the West Midlands from the larger city centre theatres to our smaller suburban theatres.

Theatres are a focus of energy as dedicated professionals and amateurs tread the boards to bring joy, laughter or even pathos to the avid theatre-goers.

Theatres across the country have numerous ghost stories attached and the Midlands theatres are no exception.

WHO IS TREADING THE BOARDS?

Suzy, a member of the Sutton Coldfield arts scene, says she has experienced unusual happenings at two of the town's amateur theatres.

She said: "In Sutton Arts Theatre when I am walking down the backstage corridor, I can feel a presence behind me and then it breezes past and pushes down the handle to the door on the way to Front of House before I can get to it. This happens very regularly.

"In Highbury Theatre, me and my partner at the time heard footsteps across the stage while we were below the stage picking up some music stands. We thought this was strange as the theatre was empty but assumed someone else had come back for something.

"When we got back up on to the stage, we realised that the theatre was empty and had been all along.

"We even called around other cast and crew to check and no one else had been in the building."

THEATRE IS A HIVE OF 'AC- TIVITY'

If the stories are to be believed, The Alexandra Theatre in Birmingham is actually home to five ghosts who might be wondering where all of the theatre patrons have gone.

In 1902 an actress called Gracie Housley died on stage and this tragedy has been linked to some of the ghostly sightings of a grey woman walking backstage.

Leon Salberg was a manager at the theatre from 1911 until 1937 when he was found dead in his office in the theatre. It is said that his spirit can still be heard and seen today making knocking sounds and jangling his keys as he walks around his beloved theatre.

The ghost of a cleaning lady has also often been seen sitting in the grand circle and walking up and down the stairs and in the auditorium.

There are also numerous reports of a former wardrobe manager who makes his presence known in the dressing rooms and also there have been reports of a man in military uniform who also prowls the many corridors and nooks and crannies of this beautiful building.

An investigation by UK Paranormal Consultants carried out an investigation and reported several unexplained phenomena, this included knocking and tapping noises were heard, doors opening and closing, batteries losing their charge rapidly and a feeling of being prodded.

GRAND OLD GHOSTS

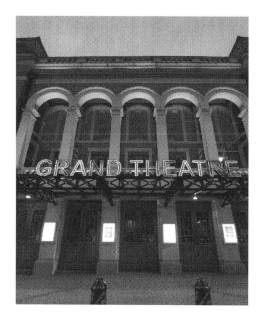

The Wolverhampton Grand has numerous stories which were sent to us by a local lady.

The theatre is around 125 years and one of the ghost is said to be that of a Percy Purdey who lived at the theatre while he managed it. After he retired he continued to live in the flat as he loved the theatre so much. Staff are used to Percy making his way through the theatre unlocking doors, moving furniture and interfering with the spirits behind the bar. They also hear footsteps and glimpse figures in the doorway. The spirit is seen as being harmless and is referred to affectionately.

The Express and Star reported that Syd Little of Little and Large, a comedy duo in the 1970s, had a very spooky experience at the Wolverhampton Grand.

Attending a party in the upstairs bar, he was directed to the nearest toilet. He said at the time: "It was all in darkness and I had a very cold feeling beside me. I had a very strong feeling that someone was there and I knew nothing about the ghost at that time. I don't believe in that sort of thing…. But I was terrified. I couldn't get out quick enough!"

BILSTON BALLROOM

John contacted us with a story from 1968.

John said: "I was not working at the time and was a member of Bilston Drama Company and I was helping build the set in Bilston Town Hall Ballroom.

"The stage was quite high and the three of us were standing at the stage looking at the drawings for the set before starting to erect it. Suddenly the swing doors at the other end of the hall swung open and we all turned to look as this middle aged man walked in, strode across the hall and out of the swing doors on the other side, we spoke to him as he passed but got no reply.

"Some time later the concierge came in to ask if we were OK and if anyone had bothered us, we told him no but added the story of this short older man in a grey suit with a white shirt and black leather shoes.

"The concierge looked puzzled and said there is no one like that who works here, I'll ask around.

"The next time we saw him (the concierge) he said that nobody knew of the man that we described but someone suggested it was the ghost of Tommy Wood the one time Mayor of Bilston . Tommy Wood had bought cinema to the town in the Ballroom we were working in before building Woods Palace opposite which then became The Odeon Bilston.

"Us three young guys then realised something strange, as we watched him walk across the empty ballroom he was wearing leather shoes but they didn't make any sound, no footsteps no shoes tapping on the floor. No sounds whatsoever except the swinging of the doors!"

STATIONS

We don't tend to linger at stations. They are a place of transition. We arrive, we might grab a coffee and a croissant and then we leave.

They can be a place though of deep joy though, greeting a family member or a friend. They can be a place of sadness as you bid farewell to a child off to university for another term.

For some, though, it feels like their stay at the station is longer than many, possibly even eternal!

DISTURBED IN THE NAME OF PROGRESS

New Street Station is the largest station in Birmingham and therefore also the busiest. Building started in 1846 and the station opened in 1854. When it opened it had the largest single-span arched roof in the world.

What many of the commuters visiting New Street Station don't realise is that platform 4 is built upon what was once a Jewish cemetery. The cemetery was situated in the garden of one of Birmingham's earliest known synagogues and in use from at least 1730. It is thought that it closed in about 1750.

It stood undisturbed for around 100 years until Birmingham City Council made a compulsory purchase order and the site was cleared. All of the bodies were moved with some being reinterred in Witton Cemetery and New Street Station was enlarged. Platform 4 sits where the burial ground once stood and accounts from across the years have reported seeing the spirits of people in orthodox Jewish clothes.

CLAUDE AND WALTER

Platform 4 at New Street Station has been called one of the most haunted places in the United Kingdom and there are numerous other reports of apparitions and ghostly bangs especially around the toilets and ticket office.

There are two ghosts who are most commonly seen in and around platform 4 they are called Claude and Walter.

Claude apparently poisoned himself on platform 4 in Victorian times. Claude is reported to be an elderly man who is particularly well dressed and very debonair. He doesn't cause any trouble, apparently he just watches people going on about their lives getting on and off the trains. He looks as solid as the next man and only stands out because of his rakish Victorian clothes and top hat.

The other gentleman is known as Walter. He was a retired train driver nursing a broken heart after splitting with his wife. He was found slumped in the waiting room at Platform 4 in 1937 after shooting himself in the heart. Sometimes he is still spotted in and around Platform

4 waiting patiently. Maybe he will find peace one day.

SPIRITUAL LI-AISON OFFI-CER

Leamington Spa Railway Station also lays claim to being very haunted. Staff and commuters had reported a number of spooky happenings which take the form of poltergeist activity. Office workers have many issues in the building which were built in the 1880s.

Papers are thrown, lights are switched on and off and doors are slammed, all by unseen hands. Lisa used to work at Leamington Spa Train station and contacted us to say that it was a very spooky place to work, especially late at night. A common occurrence was to hear heavy footsteps behind you only to turn around and find no-one there. In fact so troubled was the building that the station employed a Supernatural Liaison Officer to investigate the ghostly goings-on!

GREY LADIES

We seem to have an abundance of grey ladies in the West Midlands. We were inundated with stories about grey ladies in a variety of settings from grand locations such as castles to a motorway roundabout.

The stories all involve an ethereal form that drifts through the environment, paying little heed to that which goes on around them?

They are chilling apparitions though and there tends to be numerous sightings making them reports that can be traced back through the years.

THE GREY LADY OF DUDLEY

The most famous of these grey ladies is the one that stalks Dudley Castle.

A castle has stood on this location since 1070 and has a long history of being destroyed and rebuilt. It is truly a place awash with ghostly stories and a popular ghost hunt location (highly recommended).

There are numerous sightings of a grey lady and they are said to be the spirit of Dorothy Beaumont. Dorothy lived at the castle during the English Civil War. After her infant daughter died she was grief stricken and died soon after. Her last request was to be buried by her daughter but due to the disruptions of the Civil War her last wishes were not followed.

The grey lady is now said to aimlessly wander the halls of the castle grounds looking for her lost husband and daughter! Interestingly, she was recently captured on a mobile phone camera image.

THE LADY IN FANCY DRESS

Our very favourite ghost story from Dudley Castle is from 1983.

The castle was running a medieval evening. Participants were asked to dress up and there were prizes for the best medieval costume. While there were many fantastic costumes the judges spotted an elderly woman wearing a sackcloth shift and grey shawl with feet wrapped in sacking. She was standing nonchalantly in the crowd.

The judges were incredibly impressed with her authenticity and after some discussion awarded her the prize. Before the prize could be given out though she mysteriously disappeared. The officials on the gates were certain that she had not slipped past and she has never been back to reclaim her prize.

Who was the mysterious lady, was she a reveller who didn't want any attention or was she a ghostly visitor from the past?

THE GREY LADY OF WARLEY WOODS

Warley Woods in Smethwick is the most beautiful green space and has the icon Dame Julie Walters as its patron. It has a long history including a building known as Warley Abbey, which was demolished in the 1950s.

There are a few ghost stories associated with this area and the most common one is the Grey Lady of Warley Woods. This lady is often seen

walking around the woods, often near where the Abbey once stood. Dressed all in grey, she is regularly seen by people who are using the woods as a shortcut late of a night.

Rumour has it that her lover was killed in a war and she is waiting for him to return home. The reports of a grey lady are found to go back to 1822. The apparition was even used as a defence in a murder trial in court when the man on trial claimed that the victim was killed when his horse was 'spooked' by the grey lady.

A sketch of her is reported to have been included in Punch Magazine and a first hand report by a child from 1906 is quite chilling: "Near the poolside, away from the beech trees, there were two big oak trees, and by these trees was the figure of a lady.

"Before we could stop him, our dog tore the lead from our hands and ran off we definitely saw the lady: she was wearing an old-fashioned dress that touched the ground, and she had a dignified manner.
"The light was not that bad, but we could not distinguish her features. She was looking straight towards us, and we began to feel very scared, so we bolted for home."

GREY LADY HITCHHIKER

A motorway island is a very busy place but a Sandwell roundabout by the West Bromwich football ground is reputed to be haunted by a grey lady.

In the middle of the island is all that remains of Sandwell Lodge which was demolished many years ago.

Apparently it is home to two ghosts. One is a hooded figure which seems quite similar to the monk who is seen on Forge Lane. However there are also reports of a ghostly grey lady.

Matt says that he saw a strange female apparition. "I was driving home from work in the early hours of the morning" he explained. "At the side of the island was a woman dressed in a long white dress. She just seemed so out of place and not paying any attention to the traffic. I was quite concerned so I went back round the island to find that she had disappeared!

"I was really spooked, there was nowhere that she could have gone, she was there one minute and gone the next!".

It is not the first time a ghostly apparition of a woman has been sighted at this island. There are reports of people pulling up to what they think is a female hitchhiker only to find that she has vanished into thin air.

Is the grey lady connected to Sandwell Lodge? Perhaps we will never know.

THE BLACK PATCH GHOSTLY LADY

The Black Patch in Smethwick is now a park but previous to that it was farmland and in the early 20th century became a campsite for Gypsies. The Gypsies on the Black Patch lived on a deep barren layer of furnace dust and debris.

Esau Smith was the king of the camp and is also referred to as King of the Gypsies. He administered Romany justice and brought order to the camp. His wife was called Henty (pictured) and she is often referred to as "Queen of the Gypsies". When Essau died in 1901, Henty was in sole charge and was very well-respected amongst them.

Sadly the Gypsies were evicted from the Black Patch in 1905 and Henty is said to have uttered a curse upon anyone who chose to build on the Black Patch.

Rumours abound that Queen Henty still strolls through the Black Patch the place that she was happiest with her king.

Mrs Heeley reported that she has seen the ghost of Queen Henty as she was walking through the park in the 1970s.

"She just appeared on front of me" said Mrs Heeley. "She was wearing a long black dress and a red cape and had beautiful long black hair for her age. She was there for but a moment before she disappeared. "

A recent sighting was from 2011 when children were playing in the park and saw a figure, again dressed in a long black dress appear and disappear as quickly as she came.

In fact there is even a folk song written about her by Bryn Phillips.

They were evicted in 1905
Their belongings were callously thrown aside
As their gardens were trampled the women cried
Their tears stained Black Patch Park
Years after the Gypsies had gone

Queen Henty was seen - her hair still black and
long
With a black dress and red cape she walked
along
A pathway in Black Patch Park

Another interesting titbit is that there is rumour
that Charlie Chaplin was born on the Black
Patch. His son even came over from France to
unveil the memorial that exists in the park for
the Gypsies that made their home there.

THE GREY AND LAVEN-DER LADY

We are heading back to the Wolverhampton Grand Theatre which also has a grey lady who is also accompanied by the smell of lavender.

"Occasionally staff also spot her out of the corner of their eye. A ghostly apparition drifting away and fading as quickly as she appeared. "

There are numerous stories as to who the ghost is. Some say a past audience member and some believe her to be a former mayoress of Wolverhampton who fell to her death from one of the boxes.

A previous staff member of the Grand said "You tend to feel the chill of her first and then there will be a distinct odour of lavender. The experiences were most often in the dress circle or one of the boxes.

HISTORIC HALLS

The landscape of the Midlands is scattered with numerous halls all holding onto their own individual part in our history.

Some lie sadly derelict like Great Barr Hall, some have been turned into museums like Aston Hall and Soho House and some have become hotels or residential homes.

There are strange tales attached to many of them and stories old and new arrived in our inbox.

GHOSTLY GREAT BARR HALL

Great Barr Hall is an old Jacobean mansion which now stands in a very sorry state of repair compared to its grandeur of old. It really does have an amazing history from family home, meeting space for the Lunar Society and then becoming the site of St Margaret's Mental Hospital.

Down from the hall is a beautiful lake and gorgeous woodland. Lady Bateman-Scott is reputed to haunt the old Great Barr Park and many claim to have seen her in white, flowing gowns, floating just on top of the lake's surface or in the space where her wonderful staircase once stood.

An old legend stated that her form once lured a young man into the waters causing him to have a mental breakdown.

A woman who worked at the hospital told this strange tale.

"I witnessed a young girl shouting one Friday night at the side of the lake and as all the patients were accounted for we finally involved the police because her pleading and begging was so intense. The following day I met a policeman in the dining room and he told me his dog refused to cross the stepping stones on the lake and that nothing untoward had been found, even though an underwater search team and tracker dogs had been investigating all night."

There are a lot of strange stories about Great Barr Hall. A security guard who worked there for a while said "It was an amazing tranquil place to work a real privilege to have the building and the grounds all to myself. Just every now and then almost as if something had just realised I was there something odd or disturbing would happen and I have no explanation."

Another local lady contacted us to say that they had been exploring the building and took some photos which she believes shows a strange grey mist in the door which wasn't there as they took the photo.

A man called Andy said he recently visited the site around 10.30pm and said he had a strong feeling of being followed. "It was a really spooky sense as I walked round. Like I was disturbing somebody even though it was totally empty apart from me."

A gentleman called Keith thinks he also saw the ghostly figure of Lady Scott riding through the Pheasey estate in the 1950s. He said "People were always saying to look out the white lady riding her horse and there I was doing my early paper round and what do I see but the ghostly white lady on her horse!"

There are also many stories of phantom horses and carriages around Great Barr Hall and there were indeed a number of carriage tracks running towards the building. Interestingly there might be a connection to another famous local hall.

PHANTOM COACH AND HORSES

Soho House was once the home of Matthew Boulton. It became a hotel and is now a museum under the curatorship of Birmingham Museums.

It is widely reported that a phantom coach and horses were often heard in the vicinity. A former resident of Soho House when it was a hotel reported that the coach and horses could be heard coming up the drive and come to a halt outside the front door but there was never anyone there. Could it be the coach and horses was transporting members of the Lunar society who met at Great Barr Hall to Soho House. During renovations, a 'besom' or broom was discovered behind a boarded up fireplace – a traditional technique used to ward off witches – in the location believed to have been occupied by warriner's hut (the watchman) of Handsworth Heath.

THE MOST HAUNTED HALL IN BRUM?

Aston Hall is also a Jacobean Mansion nestled within the very urban area of Aston and a stone's throw from Aston Villa football ground.

It is breathtakingly beautiful and well worth a visit. It also has a rich and varied history, full of tragedy and intrigue and one of the staircases is still damaged from a cannonball fired during the civil war.

Obviously with stories of great suffering come ghost stories and Aston Hall has many of them. Two of them revolve around Thomas Holte who was a previous owner of the hall.

Thomas Holte does not come off well historically and is reported as being a cruel and difficult man. He disowned a son due to his choice in marriage and when he found out his daughter was planning to do the same he was furious. On finding out his daughter planned to elope and marry without permission he locked her away in a small bedroom near the servants quarters for 16 years. This entrapment sent her slowly mad before her untimely death. It is said that the grey lady ghost that is repeatedly seen is her ghost trapped within the majestic walls of Aston Hall to perpetually walk in torment. Thomas Holte sounds to be a terrifying man. Rumours abound that he murdered a chef with a meat cleaver.

Another tale is that a servant boy was accused of stealing food from Holte. He was held in a room in Aston Hall to await the wrath of his master. He was so petrified of the punishment that he hung himself and the room is now called "Dicks Garret". His spirit is seen around Aston Hall, wandering the dark corridors.

Aston Hall organise regular ghost hunts and we received a story from someone who went on one such hunt.

Jenny said " We were walking round the hall and it was dark and very atmospheric.

"The last place we visited was Dicks Garret which is a sad little bedroom which makes you feel even sadder when you hear the terrible story. I was standing with my back to the door when I felt a cold finger gently stroke my neck. It absolutely chilled me to the bone and I could not get out of there fast enough!

"There was no-one behind me and I am convinced it was a spirit."

Jenny added "My friend took a video of the space by Dicks Garrett and its absolutely full of orbs. We tried to isolate a frame to show the orbs streaking past at the corner of the bed."

137

HIGHWAYMEN

We certainly were not expecting stories about but it seems that our local area is a bit of a hub for such things.

Highwaymen rode on horses and would work in small groups or alone. They preyed on travellers in carriages or on horseback. People travelling between cities and towns were targeted and usually provided rich pickings of cash and jewellery and it proved a profitable yet dangerous trade.

They have gained an almost romantic tradition but in fact they were a real scourge and roads around Sutton Coldfield were described as being particularly dangerous by a Venetian visitor in 1497.

NEW HALL CAVALIER

New Hall is the oldest moated hotel in the UK and has a huge share of history. At the time that Cannonballs were being shot through the banister at Aston Hall, New Hall was also the backdrop to the English Civil War.

New Hall is said to be home to the very elegant ghost of cavalier in a velvet suit, complete with neck ruff, matching black patent leather shoes set-off by gleaming buckles. The cavalier is spotted in the grounds and also in the building.

It is not known whether this cavalier met a grisly end as there is also a persistent tale that the noise of a horse drawn carriage said to contain a Cavalier making his escape from Roundhead pursuers thunders down the Yew Tree Walk.

SPOOKED ON THE SOFA

A lady wrote to us to tell us about her aunt who lived in Kingstanding. She said "My Aunt told us this story many times as it really scared her and stayed with her for her whole life.

"It was a few years ago when it was customary to have sofa placed away from the wall. She was sitting on the wall when totally unexpectedly a highwayman started to appear through the wall at the back of the sofa.

"She was frozen in fear as he walked around from the back of the sofa. He looked directly at her but his face was in shadow as his hood was pulled up over his head. He moved round the sofa, bent down to my aunt and swept his cloak over her, and as he did so he disappeared!

"The experience left my auntie considerably shaken and she had no doubts that it was a real apparition."

PHANTOM RIDERS

We have also received information about ghostly horse riders having been seen around Kingstanding Circle in the past and causing motorists to have accidents.

Drivers would be navigating the island only to come suddenly across a man riding on a horse.

In the panic to avoid them they would swerve and have an accident only to find the horse and rider had completely disappeared.

It became a common occurrence around The Circle in the 1960s/1970s.

CHESTER ROAD

We received a story from a gentleman called Roy.

"Late one night I was driving up the Chester Road, by the Hardwick Arms. The road was really quiet and I couldn't see anyone else around. Unexpectedly, out of nowhere came the thundering sound of horse hooves!

"They were going really fast at what I would describe as a gallop. I put my brakes on, looked in all my mirrors, but there was nothing to be seen.

"The sound stopped as quickly as it came but I had to pull the car over and catch my breath. The hooves were pummelling the ground so fast and I was in a bit of a panic as I just couldn't work out where it was coming from!"

BOLDMERE GIBBET

We came across another story about a haunting in Boldmere. A family reported that their child was sitting innocently eating breakfast when she said "Mummy a glass man with a funny hat came to the end of my bed last night."

The family reported that this was a regular occurrence and sometimes they would hear noises like nails being hammered into wood.

Over the course of 30 years the noises and sightings became a backdrop to family life and sometimes it would stop for a while.

When it returned again in 2003 the family decided to do some research. After consulting old maps and deeds, the family discovered that one of Sutton's oldest relics, the gibbet - or hanging stone was just yards from their garden.

It was the site where, in the 18th century, highwaymen, murderers and even petty thieves were put to death, before being left to hang for all to see.

TIME SLIP?

There is a more recent story of a woman who was on the island by the Cat and Fiddle on the way up to Barr Beacon.

She looked across and saw three men who looked like Highwayman sitting on three chest-nut coloured horses! The highwayman closest to her turned his head to her and looked directly at her.

He seemed to be as confused as the woman and then suddenly the world came back to normal! No-one else in the car noticed anything but the woman was convinced.

After this story was released in 2009 there were a number of other people that came forward to say they had also seen these strange highwaymen and that they looked so solid and real that they wondered if it was a historical re-enactment society.

GHOSTLY ANIMALS

Spirits might not just be of the humankind and there are many stories of ghostly animals and not just highwaymen with their trusty steeds.

Pets become part of the family and part of the routine and we had a number of stories about family members who thought their cat was in the room, only to remember they had passed away recently.

We also collected some stories about strange creatures, or cryptids as they are known.

CLEVER CAT

Sarah wrote to us to say "We lost our beloved cat a few years ago but still remember him fondly as he was such an intelligent cat.

"About a week after he died, my partner called to me from the other room. When I got there he had a strange look on his face and he said that he had just felt something rubbing around his legs and ankles like our cat used to do.

"When he looked down, there was nothing there. It may just have been wishful thinking but we like to think that it was a final farewell from our best little buddy."

THE FOX OF COSELEY MOOR

Church bells ringing at midnight made Elaine from the Black Country wonder whether there had been more to an encounter with a red fox than she realised.

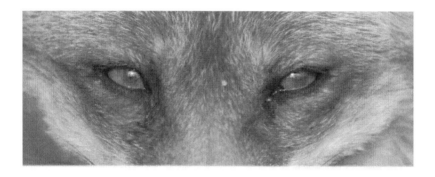

She explains that on an ordinary day in summer, where all the colours of the paving slabs are comfortingly the same and nothing was unusual in her quiet part of the world, something very unusual happened.

"Warm sunlight filtered down as if it was a luminous starfish suspended high above. I turned the corner at the top of the road and walked almost to the top of Oak Street until I stopped to listen to the swaying grasses that were enjoying themselves in the mellow breeze.

"They whispered to me: 'Come hither, come hither' as if hypnotised. I stepped through a small opening divided by a low rustic fence that looked like it was waiting for a pony to jump over it and trot around Coseley Moor, for that was where I was; this beautiful green handkerchief of wild flowers and dots of buttercups was Coseley Moor.

"The magnetism of the sun and the golden breeze led me further in, I trod almost gently as if I might hurt the grass and there it was... a shining red fox. It immediately looked me in the eyes with piercing charm, all in a moment. This red fox seemed like a statue, fixed to the ground, or even like a cardboard cut-out that had lost its way from the circus fair. We were both started."

Elaine says they stepped back and moved away from each other. She carried on with her day, the meeting with the fox playing on her mind.

"Gradually, the crowds crept into the night until it grew dark," she added. "I looked up at the moon and I heard a church bell chime, 12 midnight chimes."

But… the church never chimes its bells at midnight.
"So, was it the antics of the Coseley Moor fox that had climbed to the top of the church roof, or was it the ghost of Coseley Moor echoing in the rustling grass?'

SUTTON PARK HAS A ROYAL VISITOR!

All of these ghost stories also lead you into interesting local history. Henry VIII had a hunting lodge in Sutton Park and it is now part of the Bracebridge Restaurant. This strange story was posted on the internet.

In 1976 the hunting lodge building was being run as a cafe by a couple.

In 1977 the lady of the couple was alone one night in bed in the cottage attached to the cafe, their Collie dog was on the floor next to the bed. The dog started to growl and backed up trying to hide under her bed. She looked towards the window of the room wondering what the dog was growling at and to her shock and surprise saw the face and regalia of Henry VIII appear.

She didn't tell anyone about the first event thinking that no-one would believe her.

A few months later another incident occurred. She and her partner had just got into bed when they both heard the noise of horses hooves coming from what had used to be the old stable block, but had now been converted into a new food kiosk.

They also heard what sounded like big boulders being rolled/ dropped in the brook which runs alongside the cafe's cellar.

A door leading from the kitchen area to the lounge was opened and they could hear foot-steps. The couple were terrified and barricaded themselves into their room and phoned the po-lice.

The police on their arrival found no signs of a break in or any footprints in the muddy ground outside.

Apparently there have been several subsequent reports of King Henry VIII's ghost being seen around Bracebridge Pool cafe and the Four Oaks Gate area of Sutton Park, his ghost has been seen by visitors to the park walking their dogs late at night in the park, courting couples, and park rangers.

In fact, the most recent report was by young lads who were riding motorbikes round by the lake who saw a fat man on a horse wearing tights, a funny hat and with a beard. This was in 2006.

BEN THE DOG

Samantha wrote to tell us about their story after their beloved dog passed. Samantha said "We loved Ben, he was a loyal and much loved member of the family and we were devastated when he died of old age.

"A few weeks after, my husband was in the kitchen when he heard Ben barking in the living room. He ran into the room only to find it empty. After this incident I would often hear him padding down the laminate floor and then remember sadly that he wasn't with us anymore.

"It did stop after a couple of months but we found it a comfort to think that Ben was still checking we were OK."

MERRIONS WOOD CRYP- TOID

Andrew wrote to us to tell us about his strange encounter in Merrions Wood. Merrions Wood on the borders of Walsall and Great Barr is a beautiful site of 12 hectares.

Andrew said he was walking through the wood about twenty years ago. "I had walked through these woods so many times, I have never felt worried or in any way concerned.

"My dog was off his lead and having a good sniff and investigation. Suddenly he stopped still and gave out a low growl. I looked towards where he was growling which was quite dense woodland and I could see a huge shadowy figure.

"It was dark and I estimate over 6ft tall and really broad. I couldn't distinguish any features but I was really fearful. My dog carried on growling and the creature started to move further away from us and the noise of the trees breaking was very loud.

" I could not get away from the area fast enough. I turned on my heel and left the same way I came dragging my dog behind me. The whole experience was probably only minutes but it felt like a lifetime and remembering it stills makes me feel cold."

Andrew finished with: " I avoided the woods for a few days after that but finally plucked up courage to return and have never experienced anything like that again!"

BLACK SHUCK ON THE BEA- CON

The Black Shuck is the folklore of a huge black dog. Legend has it that Black Shuck prowls along dark lanes and lonesome field footpaths.

If you were unlucky enough to see Black Shuck then it was a harbinger of death. He was said to have fiery eyes, a blood curdling howl but soundless footsteps.

There is a story collected by West Midlands Ghost Club about an enormous black dog with bright red eyes that was seen on Barr Beacon.

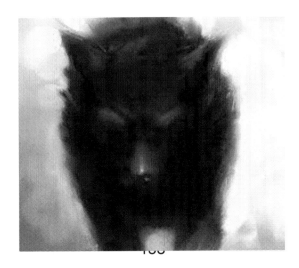

Three family members had been returning home from an evening out when the path of their car was blocked by an enormous, black dog. It was so large they wondered if it was a calf but they realised it was something far more sinister, with bright red eyes and seemed to fear nothing. After around 30 seconds the dog dis-appeared and the car and its occupants could carry on with its journey.

Cannock Chase also has a famous black dog which is known online as the Hellhound. The hound has been seen many times walking along the roads leading into Cannock and Huntington.
Similar to the Barr Beacon sighting, it is said to be large and black with fiery eyes. The sightings peaked around the 70s and 80s.

WORKPLACES

When we imagine ghosts, we might think of the traditional haunted mansions or spooky castles but judging by the range of stories, ghosts can be anywhere.

We received a number of stories about ghosts being present in the workplace from factories to hotels to pubs.

FORKLIFT
SPOOK

Gordon used to manage the night shift at his factory that made trains. He wrote to tell us about this strange little story in a local factory.

Gordon said "It was a perfectly normal night until one of the workers came screeching over to the office on his forklift truck.

"The worker had been driving his forklift truck over at C-Shop and looked down to see another member of staff walk past him. The forklift driver offered a greeting and then realised that the man who had just walked past him had died a few years ago!

"The man driving the forklift was utterly terrified and rushed back to the office to report what he had seen. He was absolutely chilled to the bone, convinced he had just seen his deceased workmate and had to have a strong cup of tea. I had to go and investigate in case it was an intruder and make a report.

"We didn't find any intruder in the factory that night but we did find the skid marks from the forklift!"

GET OUT OF MY BED

Lucy who is from the Midlands was on a business trip and staying at Buckden Towers.

Lucy said she was fast asleep when she dreamt that a man was trying to wake her up.

"He seemed cross that I was sleeping in his bed" said Lucy. "The man was wearing thick flannel pyjamas with a really strange collar. I know it sounds terrible but I told him to go away and it stopped. The next morning I thought it was quite an odd experience and I told a few people but pushed it to the back of my mind and carried on with the seminar.

"When I got home I did some research into Buckden Towers and discovered that during the First World War, the house was used as a convalescent hospital for soldiers returning from the front.

I remembered the strange pyjamas that this man was wearing. On doing more research I found that soldiers in hospitals were issued with a convalescent soldiers' outfit. This outfit was made of a flannel and flannelette combination, and its lounge-jacket counterpart resembled ill-fitting pyjamas.

"That finding chilled me to my bone and I really cannot explain this strange dream, why the details were so detailed and matched with historical details which I had absolutely no knowledge of prior to the encounter."

LITTLE GIRL GHOST

Marion contacted us with a story also from a night away in a hotel.

Marion said " My Mom and I were staying in an old hotel in Beverley, Yorkshire. We were there for a family Christening. The first night I was woken up with a tap on my shoulder, I turned over to see a little girl standing by my bed she smiled and said hello and then she was gone.

"She was dressed in a very old fashioned dress like a pinafore dress and had ringlets. I didn't feel frightened and the next morning I decided it was a very old building and assumed she had an association with the building.

"Later that day I was telling the story to my Mom. She went very quiet. My Mom was living with me at the time (in Walsall) and my mom said she has also seen this little girl ghost but strangely in my house! .She hadn't told me in case I was worried!

"We tried to think who it could be and decided that it might be a family member who had passed away many years ago. We never saw her again though."

SCRAPYARD GHOST

Scrap metal company Taronis in Aston reported persistent haunting experiences in the office buildings in 2015.

Temperatures drops in the office rooms were reported along with documents being thrown all around the place and weird bangs and noises. Employees also reported seeing figures coming out of the walls.

Worryingly the building was also left flooded after a toilet was smashed to pieces when no-one was in the building. The business insist the building was locked and and alarmed and they can offer no explanation as to how this happened.

The manager said "There's definitely something going on. You go up there and the temperature drops so much you have to catch your breath. We've been here six years and when the previous owners visited, their first question was, 'have you seen the ghost ?'"

The ghost was also photographed staring out of the window.

AFTERWORD

We hope you have enjoyed reading our book. If you have any stories you would like to share then please email us on.

burnhartpublishing@gmail.com

We are particularly interested in stories around pubs, cafes and hotels as we want this to be the next subject of our next book.

www.burnhartpublishing.co.uk

ABOUT THE AUTHORS

Louise Blackburn and Charlotte Hart

With the arrival of Covid19, Louise Blackburn and Charlotte Hart, who both originate from Birmingham, unexpectedly found themselves in very different situations to the ones they were in six months earlier, Now both married in their early 40s, they have been friends since primary school. They have often talked about working together on a book...Then, a change in the world and more time on their hands meant they finally found themselves at a point when a new challenge felt right.

THANK YOU
FOR READING

Printed in Great Britain
by Amazon